FRACTURED LENS

Vijaya Sundaram

Červená Barva Press
Somerville, Massachusetts

Červená Barva Press
P.O. Box 440357
W. Somerville, MA 02144-3222

www.cervenabarvapress.com
Bookstore: www.thelostbookshelf.com

Cover art: Courtesy of cottonbro studio
Pexels.com

Cover Design: William J. Kelle
Production: Steve Asmussen

ISBN: 978-1-950063-66-6

CONTENTS

Acknowledgements

Friends and Supporters:

Rob Bethel introduced me to Gloria Mindock. Thank you both for seeing something in my poetry that moved you. Shobha Prasad, my best friend from teenagehood, is one of my earliest readers and supporters. Thank you for your love and support, Shobha. I am also deeply grateful to Bonnie-Ann Black, James Bryant, Poppy Charnalia, Michelle Kisliuk, Kalyani Krishnan, Ilene Lerner, Alexandria Levin, Milva McDonald, Milind Mulick, Cathleen Reed, Susan Reich, Suraja Menon Roychowdhury, Kalpana Sarathy, Cortney Skinner, Padma Sridhar, and Benjy Wertheimer – thank you all for your love, friendship and encouragement.

I'm grateful to Terry E. Carter, Medford's First Poet Laureate, for sharing poetry and space with me and other Medford poets, and for encouraging us all, and to Glenn Dickson, for inviting me to do my first poetry-music performance with him on a Mass Cultural Council Local Arts Grant.

Teachers:

I wish to thank poets Elizabeth McKim, who is my first real mentor in poetry, and Judith Steinberg, whose teaching through Teachers as Scholars has been a source of inspiration. I am grateful to poet Richard Cambridge for his staunch support for the past few decades. Going further back, I remember Sister Leena, of Holy Angels Convent, who recognized and quietly encouraged my love of poetry (and with whom I shared a love of Wordsworth), and Mrs. Sathyanathan, my 8th Standard English teacher, who shared her love of literature with us, and recognized the poet inside an unfashionable, two-plaited, teenager.

Tʜese beings are near to my heart. I dedicate this book to:

Kamala Sundaram, my mother, who inspires me endlessly, and without whom I probably wouldn't have learned to read; Usha Sangam, my sister, and Rammohan Sundaram, my brother, for their love, support, and loyalty; Warren Senders, my husband, heart of my heart, music teacher extraordinaire, inspirer of all things wonderful in everyone around him; Sharada Sundaram-Senders, our daughter, who brings beauty, song, light and joy into our lives; and Holly, our standard poodle, whose uncomplicated love and trust is a deeper motivation than she will ever know.

FRACTURED LENS

Prism-me

Light trapped in crystalline form
Hanging from my window
Scatters my attention.

I climb inside teardrop-shaped
Pendalogues, and bind myself
To their empty spaces.

I could do this forever, while
Ignoring the piled-up dishes awaiting
My mindless ministrations;
The piled-up papers awaiting my
Critical and loving pen;
The coiled-up impatience of the dog
Awaiting my loving attention.

Practical matters take up room
In a dreaming mind, pierce,
And scatter focus
In multi-directional prisms,
And I would that I could
Drop everything, daring
The universe to throw anything
My way, knowing I could toss it back.
It'd be a game of catch.
And no one would lose.

I wish I could go under
The surface of things,
Go through the inner and outer layers

From one plane to another,
And breathe, gill-breathe,
All that lies within, and without,
And which would otherwise drown me.
Gill-breathe, and swim upwards
In an entirely different direction,
Far from all I know.
I long for gills in a dry world.

Agape for Love

So much happens between what you say,
And what they hear,
It's a wonder we don't all fall into an
Abyss of non-understanding.

You look, you observe, you speak, you verbalize,
You gesticulate, you explain, you emphasize,
You expatiate, you expound, you clarify.

You do everything you can to be understood.
And the gulf between you and the Other
Sits there, like an infant with
Mouth agape, tonsils bared,
Wailing into the void.
And yet, you persist.

You speak, you explain, you expand, you expound,
You expatiate, and you expend energy, and
All your expression, knowing that even a crumb
That falls into that abyss
Will stave off hunger.

The abyss is always hungry to understand,
And always agape for love.

SHELL-LIFE

Some days, one becomes a shell.
The creature that used to be within, is elsewhere.
This is oddly interesting.
One picks it at. There's some pain.
The scab is fascinating –
All scratchy and rough, but slick with memory,
Like snail-trails leading somewhere,
But no one knows quite where, or why.

On some days, one could face
Nothingness with ease.
Would the shell then get back to being elemental?
Make a garden grow?
Adorn a god's desk?
Becoming elemental again –
How soothing that would be!

Death needs no drama, no fuss.
It just flows along, doing its job.
So does life, busy doing hers.
So, I'll get on with it –
For I've some swimming to do,
Before I find my shell again.

Here's the Thing

Here's the thing about children
In detention centers, abandoned,
Sick, dying, separated
From all that is good:

One cannot make poetry from it.
One cannot make art from it.
One cannot make anything from it.
For it is unimaginable.

It is an offense against humanity.
It makes all other emotion hollow.
It makes it hard to live
A life that holds meaning.

All joys and sadnesses become muted
When set against it.
And yet, we struggle on,
Stupid, stupefied, stunned by it all,
Still laugh, still eat and drink,
Still find pleasure in daily things.

For, if only sorrow and horror define us,
What's left?
So, we make music and art, and we sing,
Even when our voices crack,
And other cracks form within.
Dual consciousness is the new burden
All of us carry, as we try and carve out
A different vision for all people,

Perhaps, a different life.
And work in what ways we can
To tilt the balance a little in favor of humanity.

And if the horror we see doesn't kill us,
The work we do might just save us all.

My Body

A body is a curious thing to possess.
I am conscious of mine as a friend
With her own blind needs,
Her own mute sorrows, her loud joys,
Her love of some fragrances, and loathing of certain smells,
Her ears that welcome all music,
Her eyes that see beyond facades
But forget to see the facade itself.

She is the entity who shares my other consciousness.
When she is out of sorts,
But *I'm* sanguine, we confuse each other,
And sometimes it's the other way around,
But mostly, we keep peace between us.
She keeps track of time,
So that even when I'm not near a clock,
She lets me know.

When I am hurt, she forces me to shut down my other self,
And attend to her.
This is as it should be.
She has given me space to live within her
And I love her and thank her for giving me room.
She is a map of my journeys,
And the road on which the journeys took place,
And her imperfections, so many, fill me
With quiet affection.

She has shed her skin so many times, and donned new ones,
And her hands, all veined, have held this earth and other hands
With love and trust, ready to give,
Even when she lost, sometimes.
Yes, she has failed me sometimes,
But then, I failed her even more.
But mostly, we are at peace.
I shall miss her when she dies.
I do not think she'll remember to miss me
At the time of her passing.

Today, With An Old Friend

Met an old friend, and true;
Saw art that spoke of light and shadow,
Of line and white space and tone and colour,
Art that flooded the mind
With reflections of reflections,
Like glass reflecting glass
In mirrors and rivers.
A walk in a park with a volcanic-red walkway
Lined with trees that drank damp air,
As we spoke of this and that.

Later, a visit with neighbors,
With family, exchanging pleasantries,
Being pious on a day dedicated to the Goddess.
This was today. It seemed right and good,
After days of rain and staying home.

The purpose of living
Is to love, but even more,
The purpose of living
Is to build layer after layer
Of memory, like glass upon glass, upon glass,
So that when the end nears,
We can plunge right through all those layers of glass
Into a place beneath and beyond, a lake, perhaps,
Layered with images of your life –
Till, going downwards through Time,
You see a space that's waiting for you.
Singular, saturated, empty,
A white space,

With no colours, and all colours,
Holding no memories,
Holding every memory,
Where you sit, eyes closed,
And dissolve into sand,
While the glass melts over you, drop by drop,
And you find that you scatter and spread out,
As you are translated into a seashore,
Even as you arise, luminous with the numinosum,
Fully formed from the sea.

SPIRAL

When you spin in a spiral
Who's to say where it begins
And where it ends?

You could go around almost forever –
A space-ship caught at the edge
Of a black hole, forever spinning,
Your molecules getting stretched
Altered, rearranged, redistributed,
So that the you that once was,
And the you that are,
And the you that will be,
Bear no resemblance to each other,
Except that all the molecules
All the atoms, the elements
That comprised you still exist,
Albeit altered and unrecognizable,
As they spin into the heart of a dense, collapsed star.

And who's to say that you won't emerge through it
Into another time, another space, another mind, as you,
Shining and incandescent,
Trail wings of flame, as you,
Transparent and dense, a paradox of Self,
Pull and push matter at will,
To form your own, pulsing,
Radiant, clean new Universe?

FISH IN AIR

Flying fish over bicycle bars,
What single thought flew like a spark
Through turgid brain and frozen blood?
What word, now vanished, formed itself
And sliced through evening traffic air,
Like an uh-oh of finality
As you struck that sidewalk
Like a cannon?
And why is it that no memory
Surfaces like a bubble on your lips?

If Death had come, it would not have hurt.
It would have been easy.
The hurt would have been for others –
Strangers, left holding your body,
Waiting for your loved ones.

I'm glad you didn't go.
Much life is left to wade through,
To swim through,
To fly through.

Hurt exists in bad-dream-space,
But you erase hurt –
You go through your life
Erasing hurt.

So that, when the end comes, you will go
With no "Uh-oh" –
You will simply fly away

Leaving breath and blood behind,
And no sorrow will attend your passing.
And you will be a memory,
Then a memory of a memory,
Then, wink out of Mind
Over other bicycle bars farther away from Now.

A Dream of Forgetting

(A Detained Child's Memory of Another Life)

Somewhere, trees stand tall
Like my Papa, who stands
Both legs apart, arms akimbo,
Staring into the distance,
Hearing the sound of hogs
Before the peace of the afternoon
Shatters into a thousand
Shards, and slices into our family.

Somewhere, water flows like
My Mama's hair rippling in the breeze,
After she's washed it,
And she's hanging up a few clothes
To dry in burning sun,
But water is scarce, and
We are scared, and we turn
To face a land that has
Plenty, so much more
Than we can dream of.

We are here, now, in this land
Of plenty, but there's none for me.
I dream and dream, to forget
The hunger in my belly,
The smell of unwashed bodies,
And the pain slicing me
Like a rough-edged knife
When I think of both my parents,
Gone, like the memory
Of a photograph in a dream.

I sit on a concrete floor,
With little ones, hollow-eyed,
Hollow-cheeked, hollow-bellied,
With no sound coming from
Open mouths, eyes dry,
All tears gone.

Somewhere, there are flowers
Pink and blue and purple,
Scenting the air, gladdening
Bees and tempting butterflies
Which dance in the air,
Lust-crazed and dizzy above them.

Somewhere, water flows like freedom,
And I dance barefoot on grass,
Full of sweetness and the
Soft murmurings of gentle insects
So full of life and quiet rhythms.

I dream.

Somewhere, my father still stands
Tall as the trees, unbending,
On another land that is green,
He whistles, and the hogs
And goats around him lie content.

Somewhere, my mother hangs up
Clothes to dry, her hair rippling
Like waves. I eat rich, soft
Tortillas, and drink cool water,
My belly full of gratitude.

SEA-SPUN

Sea-glass, driftwood, seaweed, spume,
Sea-shells, mussels, jellies bloom.
Sunlight, moonlight, glints outbid
By algae, jellyfish, sea-worms, squid –
Fill her human eyes with longing.
Make her dream of sea-belonging
Though her sea-arms aren't quick,
Though her feet can't seem to kick,
Though the deeps fill her with fear
Though the distance tempts her near,
Still, she watches from the cliff, and
Stills her heart, approaches, stands,
Far away, a whale-song brings her
To the brink. She sings an answer.

LEARNING TO EVOLVE

You drown again, then emerge,
Delphinine, into the air,
Twisting and turning,
And sleep eludes you, you think,
But you dream, and dream, and dream,
Until your waking is a dream of waking,
And your dreaming a dream of waking.
And you walk on water, towards a distant shore
Where sylphs gather in the air, and dryads
Behind trees, and salamanders dancing
In flames that do not scorch, cool fire!
And they await you, Undine,
As you come closer, closer.

You reject the world of waking.
It is dull, plastic, a mere imitation,
Where you've loved, and lost,
And regained everything and everyone
A hundred times over.
You laugh, as the waves part beneath your
Extremities, which you cannot see,
Because you never look down, just up,
Just around, because there's so much to see,
But, as you approach land,
The droplets flying off your slick, silken skin,
You wonder, briefly, about the element
From which you came, and,
Fighting the impulse not to do so,
You look down.

Below, you see all the faces of all
Whom you left behind, all who loved you,
Or were indifferent to you, or hated you,
Or whom you didn't even know,
And even as you catch their startled
Fearful faces gazing up at you
Emerging from their world,
Poised to escape, to desert them,
The waters start rising upwards,
Until you find yourself sinking, sinking.

Waving to the dryads, the sylphs,
The salamanders, you let out a loud
Gasp, before you drown,
Once again in the world beneath.
Awake now, you find yourself
In the clutch of dry land,
Dry as hate, dry as death.
And you suck in a lungful
And learn to evolve.

Ruby-Song

I crave rubies in my throat
So I can sing like a clarinet.

The pomegranate in my fridge is tired
I regard it with fondness –
My partner in enervation.
Its redness is beyond the price of rubies.
It calls to me coldly, like a clarion,
A question shaping its urgent need.

Somewhere else, a beet sings of redness too,
Far beyond my ken, I'm sure of it,
But it sings a darker red, a sombre passion.
I will seek it at some other point.
I have need of clarity, coldness, red fire.
And this other, pressing matter at hand –
My pomegranate – which has but one purpose,
Since its other purpose was abrupted
When it was cut down from the mother-tree.

I will answer its call, but not now.
Tomorrow, I shall cut into it, inhale
Its weary fragrance, suck its tart juices.
The pomegranate will bleed in delight,
And die on my tongue.

And I will sing with a voice like rubies.

PASSING

Everything passes, even this feeling,
Everything passes, and I mourn it all,
In the impermanence there is immanence,
And when they pass – all things, all loves, all lives,
I mourn them all, and the Godhead in them.

I mourn backwards through time.
All the things I remember, and all I don't:
The whistle-lollipops on which I, a child,
Would suck with a relish I cannot recapture,
The enormous trees up which I shinnied,
Agile as a monkey, or an imp, in childhood,
The green tamarinds I ate, sour and succulent,
Hanging off branches in Pune's woods,
So mysterious, so alluring to a child,
Who never wanted to read or write,
Just play, and live in make-believe all day long.

I mourn backwards through time.
The passing of my school days,
That I valued my life so little that
I cannot remember much of it,
Only the sensory world in which I swam.
And those things I do remember,
Fill me with a spiky regret:
Sharp winter air in Pune when I was seven,
The slipping of sunlight and rain
Over polished mango leaves,
The songs on All India Radio,
The world of books into which I plunged

After my first reluctance and rejection of them,
My mother's fragrant foods which were a fact of life,

Like love, or joy, or goats on the street,
Or bird-song, or jasmine flowers at my window.

I mourn backwards through time.
But these days, I also mourn these:
The stores that close down,
Billboards which would stare down
At me while I paid them no heed,
Now gone, given way to unbearable gloss,
The decor in banks I used to visit,

Now so clinical and perfect
Like mannequins with no skin pores.
I mourn lost bookstores
In Arlington,
Or Harvard Square,
Or Porter Square,
Or Davis Square,
Or Medford Square.
I mourn the missing street performers,
Jugglers and puppeteers,
Story-tellers and singers,
We're all gone now.

I mourn the minutes, hours, days, years
Of my life, the lives of those I love,
The lives of those whom I have not yet met,
The lives of all the creatures vanishing
Before I shall ever meet them.

Everything passes through me,
And through you – and somewhere,
We'll meet, you and I, you with your
Memories, I with mine,
And we will let them flow through us,
And beyond, until all fades away.

Coming Home

(At Sanders Theatre Today)

In the dim recesses of the room,
Lights shine like forgotten memories
Surfacing among wood and metal.
Voices fill spaces and vaulted ceilings,
And the wood swallows up
All the songs, and hugs them close.
People cluster close, and their voices
Ring like vast gongs struck by lightning,
And the wood gathers them up.

My guitar is like this.
My guitar grew with my voice
Year after year, so that when
My voice was lost, I found it hiding there.
So it is with you when you are lost.
You'll find yourself over and over again
In unexpected places. So, keep looking.
Forget compasses and stars.
Forget directions and maps.
Do this when you're lost:

Find an old room you love, sit there,
Gather the air close, and sing in
All of your lost selves.
The wood remembers, the wood
Always remembers.
And all the molecules of sound
That cradled you from you birth
Will cluster close around you,
So that even when you carry your breath
From your birthplace to that foreign land,
You'll always come home.

In The Dementia Unit of the Nursing Home

I have no words tonight,
None that would suffice, anyway.
I want to be pure and simple –
Simple in thought, word and deed.
The humming of the world increases
In this room, this bed, this confined space.

A lifetime can be summed up thus:
I lived, grew older, fell, moved, died.
Perhaps, the world was changed by me
Perhaps, I was changed by it.
It matters not, not now. At present,
I am content-not content with these:

This bar of chocolate, this clementine,
These earrings, this necklace, this ancient
Gold watch that belonged to my mother's mother,
That ring, my mother's engagement ring,
These paintings, full of life and colour,
And talent – mine, my joy in seeing beauty –

These reminders of someone, a stranger
Who lived long ago, vibrant and witty,
Full of ambition and love of poetry,
Pretty and scholarly, and generous
Sarcastic and hurtful, not always liked,
Always striving to do what was right.

Rain comes down like regret,
And I forget why, although I weep.
The silent woman seated in the other bed
Speaks, and is silent again, staring fixedly at
The silent television, its screen dark.
Perhaps it's raining where she sits, too.

The Before and the After

There is no up, there is no down
Just empty space all around
And you in it, alone, floating,
Floating like nothing you could know,
Because you haven't seen it yet.

You float, unseeing, unknowing,
Quiet, and light as snowflakes,
In a place that knows none,
Where to say the word is to
Make it come true, to take a form
Where it didn't exist before.

Nothing to touch you
Nothing to hold you
No one else, but you –
Floating, floating quietly.

You cannot know you have arms
You do not know about legs
You were fed just enough,
Your stomach makes no sound, as it
Sleeps, quiet, satiated.
There is no want here.
No need.
No lack.
No greed.

Perhaps, you can hear your heart beat
Perhaps, you feel a pulse.
You cannot be sure of anything,
Not your body, not your mind.
Nothing true, nothing false,
Nothing to obscure,
Nothing to divulge.

You float in deep red
A red so deep, it's black
Sometimes blue.
Sometimes, violet,
You cannot see it, of course.
Your eyes aren't open.
The redness feels like blood.
The blackness feels like death
The blue, an entire mother, an ocean
Cradling, holding,
Caressing you.

But you can't feel it of course,
Maybe you sense it, maybe not.
You're out here, drifting, floating,
This is it, you alone, forever.
With a glimpse of the you that you are.
You feel no resistance
To the you that you are.

You float, forever.
There is no curiosity
To know the you that you are
Perhaps, there's no need.
No one else exists.
You are all of it.
This is all there is:
An imprisonment.
A release.

Firefly, or Star

Sometimes, just sometimes,
I wish I could be a stick figure.
I'd watch myself walk into the horizon.

I would reach the vanishing point
In your eyes, and my own.

Or, I could draw myself into, and
Out of existence – that would be fun.

That would be so painless
And give me such pleasure.

An Escher hand sketching itself,
Then, unsketching in a loop that unloops.

No third parties involved,
No blame, and no shame.

I would then know exactly
When to wink out of existence,
Like a firefly, or a star.

Xanadu

Daffodils light up the sidewalk
And tulips, crimson and purple
Struggle into awareness.
Trees exhale a sigh, glad
At the chance of a rebirth.
Every day is a "Why," followed
By its wry sibling, "Why not?"
And I sigh over their squabble.

I have no truck with things that trick the mind,
But sometimes, I wonder,
If someone came to my door,
Like the Person from Porlock,
Would I forget my story
And my song, even with clear-eyed,
Unclouded mind?

Would I welcome that which
Would interrupt what I had barely begun?
Would I, with song and words, build
That octagon with towers,
People it with spirits,
Hedge it about with impassable things,
And sit within, guitar in hand,
Singing of things never heard
Of places never seen,
Of people never loved?

Would my floating hair and flashing eyes
Keep you, and you, and you, at bay?
Would I look in a mirror,
And see everything, all of you,
Laterally inverted, flat, unknowable,
And know with a hard, metronomic pulse
of knowledge
That I could never know
What was real
And what was its reflection?

No Words for This

Pretty and perfect, the poem sits,
Pert, legs crossed, poised,
Breathing lightly,
Looking out on a cool,
Blue-gold, sunny Spring day.

There is no room to admit
The horrors without.
There are no words to spell
Out the voiceless O of sorrow
And unending rage.

There are no metaphors
To cover over the broken
Bodies of children
Tied, assaulted, murdered.

Meanwhile, lines of people
Leave, a cat or dog in a crate
Carried in one hand,
A suitcase, or a trunk in the other.

Buildings smoulder,
Open to the sky,
Car on fire,
A man gunned down,
Even as his arms were up,
His wife, shot in the car,
Their child parentless.

Will that child ever come back from this?
Will we ever come back from this,
From all the horrors of this broken world?

Children, broken and hurt,
Crushed beneath a brutal burden,
Will return, all aflame,
Ghosts all, translucent, screaming,
Seeking their destroyers.
And they'll consume this earth.

We did not protect them.
We do not deserve them.

The poem sits, looking at everything,
Then turns away.
There are no words for this.
There are only metaphors
For another poem about renewal.
And beautiful imagery about growth,
With Spring, waving tentatively
From another latitude.

It's cold outside.
Time to go within.

WOUND

No one tells you this:
When people die, or are killed,
All the displaced air where they stood
And breathed in and out –
All that air swirls in vortices,
Then settles, a low hum
Of loss and longing.

There's a wound, a rent
A tear, a rip in the space and time
They occupied on earth.
We patch over them, sure.
We cannot forget, though.
They are here, so present,
So wistful, so full of longing.

So vivid in memory, in our senses,
They laugh or shout,
Or whisper words, which we hear still.
Their changing face –
Caught in our minds, perhaps captured
On digital devices, or older tape recordings,
On photographs, on paper, on artwork –
Everything we experienced of them
Lingers in the folds of our memory.
They linger, full of yearning.

The air is wounded
And tries to repair itself
Over and over, busily trying
To fill in gaps, these interstitial
Spaces, so full of yearning.

Things are never the same.
They will never be the same again.
Still, we pour and pour
Something into those spaces
Which we will never refill –
Spaces, so full of longing.

Listening to Satie's Gymnopédies on an April Afternoon

The music weaves its moody way
Through rainy streets on October evenings,
Through sunlit streets on August afternoons,
Through gas-lit scenes on November nights.

The music weaves, a careful drunk,
And pauses – at a flower cart, a tram,
A motor car, some men in black coats, and women in furs,
A child and mother, a cafe on the street-corner,
A man feeding pigeons on a lonely park bench,
Some horses pulling a carriage –
Pauses, then meanders through back alleys.

Hidden behind these red and yellow-gold bursts of light,
Who knows who is lying in a gutter drunk, or dying,
Who knows who sits behind a church with sore feet and dirty face,
After selling newspapers to take home a few coins
To pay for bread and milk, some coal or wood?

That's not for us to ask, is it?
Not for those who listen, entranced,
To a piano spilling liquid notes, light rain
On street-lit puddles,
So beautiful, that our gaze is drawn upward towards
The source of that light?
We know the gutter is there.
Still, we turn our faces upwards.
The surface of the puddle shines.
We look up, seeking the source,
Even for a few minutes.

On Listening to "Dido's Lament" for the Nth Time

Why does hearing a song
about a story in Greek and Latin mythosphere,
Then, retold in English
make me, an Indian woman, weep?

Purcell makes my pulse
dissolve in a sea of sadness.

I come from the land of
loss and suffering
I come from the land of
mythology and dreams
I come from the land
where mythological princes
went into exile,
lost their loves,
learned about suffering,
found God in the midst of it all,
returned to their love,
or had their love returned to them:
There was hope there.

This song is pure sorrow.
and pure sorrow is hard
so hard to bear.

We hide behind hope
Tremble behind tropes,
Clichés, happy endings
To stories we seek

hungry for something
we know not what.

We know that in the end,
such endings are scant, for
everything ends in death,
even love.

Yet Dido sings, broken,
burning with love and betrayal,
giving up all for one
who deserves nothing,
a narcissistic, uncaring ass.

There's something beautiful
something absurd, unjust,
unfair, unbearable, about such love.

It has nothing to do with the man she loves,
and everything to do with Dido.

"Where's your dignity, woman?"
I want to cry out to her across Time
and mythos.

"You undo all that women should be,"
I want to tell her,
my voice stern and accusing.

There's another part, though,
where I admire her.
I will never emulate her,
but I ask myself, often:

What must it be like
to turn to ashes with lust,
to die for love?

Them, Theirs

Young people everywhere
Like saplings, rooted,
Yet reaching up and out,
Yearning for what they
Cannot name at first,
Then, find each other in relief.

She/Hers/Her
He/His/Him
They/Their/Them
A profusion of pronouns,
A garden of genders
A confusion of categories
A clarification of classifications
A claiming of space to live
To learn, to grow, to seek,
To be left alone to think
And love, and learn.

Leave people be!
There's enough sorrow, enough hate
Enough loss, enough lack, enough war,
Enough greed and rage to grapple with.
Leave them be, and love them.

Love and live, and laugh and leap,
Gender-bound, and gender-unbound.

Bring your loaf of bread, and jug of wine,
Sit beneath these spreading boughs,

This garden could be paradise enow,
If you remember there's space for all.

...

If we let go of greed and fear,
Let go of boxes in our minds,
All neatly labeled in the attic,
We could unpack, reveal, and air
Everything that's been sealed.

Once, before moving, I packed a box
Labelled it absent-mindedly
"Stuff in Box."
My husband still teases me about it.
I don't mind.

I like the mystery of "Stuff in Box."
I like to find things,
See a kind of History,
Herstory, Theirstory in them.
You should, too.

Catching, Holding

Reaching into the future,
The ivy catches onto things:
Little chandelier at the window;
Harlequin asleep on a crescent moon,
Holding onto a bell;
Glass star, angular, unforgiving,
Softened by a circle of brass;
The kind, but sadly-named philodendron –
Whatever catches its attention
Whatever is close by.
All it does is hold on.
It's what it can do.
That is all it knows.

I could draw a parallel,
But I'll stop here.

ERASURES AND ILLUMINATIONS

There's a moment when
You see all people:
Transparent, opaque, whole, broken, strong,
Helpless, accepting, resisting, loving, hating,
Certain, bewildered, testing, winning, losing,
Inchoate, done.

And you know –
As surely as you know that it's air you breathe,
That it's water you drink,
That it's sleep that overtakes you at night –
You know that they are all waiting
For something.

(We are all waiting.)

That they all need something.
(That we all need it.)

Helpless children we are –
We seek to sneak back unseen
To the Mother, she who kept us well-hid
Before we were born,
Tethered to her belly button.

And we see the aches, the fears,
The loves, the doubts, the rage
And disappointments
In the faces around us,
Clear as lake water near

A rocky shore, wavy with weeds
Going deeper down, while on the surface,
Reflections arise from the hills around.

It's all right there, in all of us,
That book –
Written for us before we had a say.
And when we do have a say,
That book rewrites itself,
And every time it does, it
Seems inevitable, like it's
Always been there.

And it's all right there,
In everyone – a map –
All the lines branching out
Become visible like firefly-lit air
When we step on those lines.

And every line we don't take,
Vanishes before our eyes,
Glimmers out of existence
Like a hurt, or an abandonment,
Forgiven in the end.

I need the map in hand
So I can ignore it.
It will give me strength
And something to hold,
While I drown in air, stand
Drowning on dry land.

I can walk only so far
In other people's shoes.
I need to walk in my own,
Chase down some fireflies,
Walk over to observe
Some branching lines,
Gaze mindlessly within
A limpid lake whose undulating stones
And receding shoreline will grind down
Erase all history, and all those
Transparent people will wink out,
Turn into vanishing lines.

Things That Distract

A wingless dragon, mouth open
Against books about esoteric things,
Sits impotently on a shelf.

From another dragon's mouth,
Emerges a woman gazing into the eyes
Of a half-faced demon, both fighting
Over a full moon behind them, all
Painted on a cloth on an old white door.

Rich brown braids tumble from red hat
Stitched to them, while a dream-catcher
Catches bad things that prowl,
Restless, ready to pounce.

Blue horse against black backdrop
Extravagantly silver-maned,
With impossible pointed feet, paces,
Unmoving, on blue walls,

And Dog on blue bed with me,
Quiet, content that I'm home,
So quiet, she's a blue-brindled C
Of stillness, of solace.

Glad of this respite,
Glad for my wound-down day,
Gladdened by endings,
I gaze blindly at all that distracts me,
While the urgency of mundane things
Drains slowly away.

LISTENING, A CONTINENT AND AN OCEAN AWAY

Aching voice, limned with longing
fills the air from a minaret.
calling all to their knees, to prayers,
to surrender their will to another's.

I listen to the radio,
busy and spellbound, both,
a continent and an ocean away,
grading student papers in early dawnlight.
This is mundane and magic work, both.

I listen, understanding something,
not understanding the call.

Not understanding
adds to mystery, moonlit and mad,
adds to fascination, fierce and febrile,
adds to a yearning for the unknown life.

Not religion, exactly.
Not even prayer.
It's the eternal call of longing
which sings in the nuclei,
hums, atomic and cellular.

We have all yearned like this —
To reduce it to romance is simplification.
This is of the spirit:
Like we want to break the bonds
of flesh, leap like flying fish

breaking water, splitting the air,
straight out of our element
and into an unknown one.

Flying straight out,
our fins become wings,
just briefly.

And just as briefly,
we become angels,
know what it's like
to reach apotheosis.

The fish lands back in water.
The coast is clear.
A memory of yearning
Lingers like mist,
then dissipates.

The muezzin continues to call.
I listen, entranced, and busy.

Box of Ashes

A box of ashes,
A lifetime condensed,
Arrives by mail.
Sorrow stands aside,
Breathing suspended.
Strange detachment!

You were once a Force
A Maker, Doer,
Fiercely living.
You, who scaled mountains,
And flew open skies,
Challenging death.

You sailed into ice
Fought fiercely for right,
Right, though alone.
Always and ever
On the edge of things,
Looking for love.

I always loved you.
That you knew, though
Memory-less.
I hope that sufficed
As you crossed that bridge
Alone, not lonely.

HUMMINGBIRD

~What happens when you try
try, try again?
Do you bang your head against
deaf walls, hoping they'll hear?

~They're walls, dammit!
don't hope, just do!

~It's all very well to be Zen about this,
about everything, really.
So, why bother?

~Because, to not do
is to die.

~What if you want to die?

~Listen! Hear those birds?
That humming? Those crickets?
The low, slow song of the planet?

Remember these things,
rejoice calmly, do not expect
anything, anything at all.

Open your ruby throat,
whirr your wings,
hummingbird, and sing.

Flowers will hear.
Other hummingbirds will, too.

Songless, Groundless

When no new songs come your way,
Do you turn to the old?
And what if the old bores you?
What then?

Songless, you stand,
Arms held high,
Pulling down the skies,
At the edge of something
Unspeakable, unsingable.

Nietzsche was wrong.
If you look too long into the abyss,
You might not see it
Staring back at you;
You might see the other side
Of the earth.
You might see the sky.
You might go blind,
Or see everything all at once.

Redefine the song.
Something else up there,
Or down there
Awaits, holding its breath,
Waiting to be spoken.

About the Author

Vijaya Sundaram currently is the Poet Laureate of Medford, Massachusetts (2023-2025). Originally from India, Vijaya is a poet, musician, singer-song-writer, and educator. Her work has appeared in the *Rising Phoenix Press, the Stardust Review*, and *TELL Magazine*. This is her first collection of poems in print. She lives in Medford, Massachusetts with her husband, daughter, and Holly, their standard poodle.